E
7:
AN

Mary Hip
Matt teading evening service

Jacob

TAKING HOLD OF GOD'S BLESSING

CWR

Sarah Evans

Acknowledgements

Many thanks to Rebecca Berry and the team at CWR for helping me make this book the best it can be. I'd also like to thank my family, my pastor and his wife, and all at my church for their support, love and prayers. Thanks also to you for choosing this book – may it bless you, encourage you, and help you grow closer to God.

Copyright © CWR 2017

Published 2017 by CWR, Waverley Abbey House, Waverley Lane, Farnham, Surrey GU9 8EP, UK. CWR is a Registered Charity – Number 294387 and a Limited Company registered in England – Registration Number 1990308.

The right of Sarah Evans to be identified as the author of this work has been asserted by her in accordance with the Copyright, Designs and Patents Act 1988, sections 77 and 78.

For a list of National Distributors, visit www.cwr.org.uk/distributors

All Scripture references are from the Holy Bible, New International Version® Anglicised, NIV® Copyright © 1979, 1984, 2011 by Biblica, Inc.® Used by permission. All rights reserved worldwide.

Concept development, editing, design and production by CWR.

Cover image: iStock / CasarsaGuru

Printed in the UK by Linney

ISBN: 978-1-78259-685-1

But Jacob's family life was then abundantly blessed. His wives produced children and in total, he had 13: 12 sons (who became the 12 tribes of Israel) and a daughter. Jacob was later reconciled to his brother Esau, and God continued to bless the family and provide for Jacob, even in his old age. His life was far from easy, but as Jacob chose to trust in the God of his father Isaac and grandfather Abraham, he began to see God do wonderful things in and through his life, redeeming even his most terrible mistakes.

Through these seven weeks of study, we will look at different aspects of Jacob's life in chronological order. We will explore what kind of man Jacob was, and the decisions he made that changed the course of history. We'll discover the highs and lows, good decisions and bad decisions – and consider what we can learn for our own lives.

Jacob's story reveals many different aspects of God's character to us. We will see how that God is our provider – Jehovah Jireh. He met Jacob's every need. The blessings He poured out demonstrate His generosity, mercy, extravagant love and Father heart for His children.

God was also Jacob's (and our) protector. He is our master, our guide, and He has plans for each and every one of us that are far greater than the plans we make for ourselves. If we abide in Him, trust Him and follow Him, He will reveal His plans to us. My prayer is that you will discover amazing things about our God, and the amazing blessings He has in store for your life.

If you are planning to use this resource to lead a small group, the Leader's Notes at the back will hopefully assist you in your preparation and time together. One key theme that runs throughout Jacob's story is that of prayer, so I would encourage you, whether in a group or alone,

to make time and space for prayer at some point in each session.

Jacob learned the importance of prayer, and how God wants us to live out an authentic, real and honest relationship with Him. We can talk to Him about anything; confess anything; ask anything. Indeed, it was by wrestling with God for His blessings that Jacob saw so many poured out over his life. I pray that, as you read, you are inspired to press in to the Lord in prayer, and dare to ask for the 'immeasurably more' that He offers us.

WEEK ONE

Jacob's beginning

Icebreaker

Try to think of some promises that God made to His people in Scripture, then note them down or discuss them with the group.

Bible Readings

- Genesis 12:1–3; 25:19–28
- Matthew 21:22

Key verse: 'Isaac prayed to the LORD on behalf of his wife, because she was childless. The LORD answered his prayer, and his wife Rebekah became pregnant.' (Gen. 25:21)

Focus: God is faithful to keep His promises to His people.

Opening Our Eyes

Given that Rebekah was 'childless' (presumably barren), Jacob's very existence is a miracle. A woman in that time and culture who was unable to conceive a child brought shame on herself and her husband – so Jacob's story begins with a married couple, apparently desperate to start a family but unable to have one.

Isaac married Rebekah when he was 40 years old. We cannot be sure how old Rebekah was, but convention dictates that she would have been younger than him. We see from Scripture that Rebekah couldn't have children, but her husband prayed for her for many years. As a married couple, they believed that God would move for them – after all, He had brought them together in the first place, which had been another miracle (see Gen. 24)!

Isaac had seen God move miraculously in his own life, and the life of his father Abraham. He knew that God would keep His promises (particularly that the descendants of Abraham would outnumber the stars in the sky), but despite all this, Isaac still had to wait at least twenty years to see his prayers answered, as Rebekah gave birth when Isaac was 60 years old.

Through those years of waiting, what Isaac and Rebekah couldn't see was that God was preparing their hearts and building their characters. Let's be encouraged – waiting for something good from God produces patience in our lives, and God's promises to us are *always* worth waiting for.

Even though this miraculous twin pregnancy was from God, childbirth itself may have been more excruciating for Rebekah given that her babies were wrestling in her womb. In her distress, Rebekah called out to God (Gen. 25:22) – and how encouraging it is for us to be able to seek God in all of our difficulties, whatever may be happening around or within us. As Rebekah enquired of God, He clearly answered, telling her that she had two nations in her womb, and that the older child's nation would serve the younger (Gen. 25:23). What a thing to carry!

Scripture tells us that the first child was born hairy and with a reddish skin tone, so they named him Esau (meaning 'hairy'). He was also called Edom (meaning 'red'). The second child, we are told, was born grasping his brother's heel, so they named him Jacob (meaning 'to grasp the heel' or 'deceiver').

The brothers grew up, and Esau became a skilful hunter, often going out into the fields to bring home supper, whereas Jacob was a mild-mannered man who stayed at home among the tents. Isaac loved Esau because of the food he brought home and prepared, but Rebekah favoured Jacob as he stayed closer to home, perhaps helping her with other domestic tasks. Favouritism and division within families is a timeless problem, leading to all kinds of other issues – and as we will see in later chapters, Jacob himself perpetuated the cycle in having his own favourites among his children.

Jacob and his twin brother Esau came into the world as a fulfilment of a promise from God to Abraham (Gen. 12:1–3). God makes promises to us, too, as His people. He has special plans and purposes for our lives – plans far better than ones we could ever dream up for ourselves. Let's keep on persevering in prayer and have faith in the promise of Matthew 21:22. And let's trust in God's perfect plans and perfect timing.

Discussion Starters

1. Think about a time when God promised you something but you had to wait a while for it to happen. How did you feel once it did arrive? Are you waiting for anything at the moment?

_____

_____

_____

_____

_____

2. What are some of the positive things that we can learn from the life of Jacob's father Isaac? How can we implement these things in our own lives?

_____

_____

_____

_____

_____

3. Why do you think persistence in prayer is important in our lives?

_____

_____

_____

_____

_____

4. Make a list of prayers that you have seen answered. How does it make you feel to see them written down?

_____

_____

_____

_____

_____

5. Why do you think God is concerned about our character? What attributes do you think He values the most?

_____

_____

_____

_____

_____

6. Have you or your friends ever experienced sibling rivalry? What tends to be the impact of this, and how can it be overcome?

_____

_____

_____

_____

_____

7. Doubts can hinder us from receiving God's blessings. Do you agree, and why?

_____

_____

_____

_____

_____

8. In the Bible, names are very important and their meanings often carry great significance. What do you think of the meaning of Jacob's name?

_____

_____

_____

_____

_____

Personal Application

When God gives us a promise, it's important not only to believe it, but to trust Him to fulfill it in our lives. It's easy to believe God and hold fast to these promises when it's only been a short time, but as the months or even years pass, we can lose heart and perhaps start to doubt that God will do as He said He would.

In these times of doubt, it's important to reflect on the Word of God to bring us comfort. The Bible is full of stories of people whom God promised something to, and things happened just as He said they would. We could consider Joseph, David or Moses, to name but a few. Why not reflect on your own times of faith and doubt? Are you in need of comfort and reassurance at the moment? Or is there someone you could encourage?

Seeing Jesus in the Scriptures

Isaac and Rebekah were not the only ones in the Bible to wait many years for a much longed-for child. For hundreds of years, God's people prayed and waited for Him to send them a Messiah. Jesus Himself is the fulfilment of God's promises to us.

Read the story of Simeon and Anna waiting to meet the baby Jesus in Luke 2:22–38. They were both promised something specific by God – who fulfilled what He had promised them – but they had to persevere and wait for many years for their promises to be fulfilled.

WEEK TWO

Jacob the deceiver

Opening Icebreaker

Have a quick look online to see if you can find the meaning of your name. Do you or anyone in your group have a name with Hebrew origins? Does your character match what your name means?

Bible Readings

- Genesis 25:29–34; 27:1–40
- 1 Chronicles 4:9–10
- Exodus 20:16
- Proverbs 12:22

Key verse: 'Then Jacob gave Esau some bread and some lentil stew. He ate and drank, and then he got up and left. So Esau despised his birthright.' (Gen. 25:34)

Focus: God wants His people to be blessed, but trying to obtain blessings by acting unrighteously will not please Him.

Opening Our Eyes

Deceive (verb): To make someone believe something that isn't true, to the deceiver's own advantage.

Just before I was born, my parents had to decide on what name to give me. My mum liked Rachel, but my dad wasn't so keen – so in the end they agreed upon Sarah. Did that change the course of my destiny? We'll see!

Throughout the Bible, names are incredibly important, and often carry a prophetic insight into a person's character. For example, take the name Jabez, which means 'pain' in Hebrew, and we see in 1 Chronicles that Jabez cried out to God to change his destiny. As another example, take Jacob's grandfather, Abraham, whose name means 'father of many' (and whose descendants God promised would outnumber the stars in the sky). So being called Jacob, which means 'deceiver', might not have painted the brightest picture for his future.

We see early on in Jacob's life how his name played a role in his destiny. The way he tricked Esau out of his birthright would have taken pre-meditation, planning and a very deliberate act of deception. In Genesis 25:29, we're told that Jacob was cooking a stew. He would have known when Esau would be coming home from a day's hunting, and that he would be hungry. In the culture of the time, the birthright went to the eldest son in the family, and even in the case of twins, as we have here, Esau was born first – and that meant the birthright would legally be his.

However, the 'birthright' that really matters in this text is the spiritual one, rather than the physical one. Jacob sought his spiritual birthright with eagerness, which is of course a good thing, but the way in which he obtained it was not righteous, and therefore would not please God. The spiritual birthright referred to the future possession of the land of Canaan and God's covenant with Abraham. Jacob, being true to his name, conned his brother into selling his birthright for a bowl of stew. It's worth noting here how Esau let go of what was rightfully his, at such a cheap price. In fact, we read that Esau 'despised' his birthright (Gen. 25:34).

Years prior to this transaction, when the twins were born, God had revealed to Rebekah that the elder of her sons would serve the younger (Gen. 25:23). Yet we see at the start of Genesis 27 that Isaac wanted to restore the blessing to his eldest son, Esau, against God's wishes. Perhaps he had condemned Jacob's deceit and wanted to reverse the apparent injustice done to Esau. He might not even have considered that he was going against God's bigger plans, or perhaps he loved Esau more than Jacob or had lost sight of what God had purposed for his sons. But either way, God *will* bring about His purposes – so to go against His plans is futile.

As we read on, Jacob lied to his father and deceived him by pretending to be Esau. He had already stolen his brother's birthright, then he stole his blessing. Esau had been betrayed *twice* by his brother. His anger was so intense that he wanted to kill him! So Jacob fled for his life.

But perhaps this was God's plan all along (in running from home, Jacob met Rachel, the love of his life!). Jacob was blessed by his father according to God's promise, and indeed he was blessed.

Discussion Starters

1. What does God say about lying (see Exod. 20:16; Prov. 12:22)? Is it always wrong for Christians to lie?

_____

_____

_____

_____

_____

2. The first deception was when Satan deceived Eve into eating the forbidden fruit. What other deceptions in the Bible can you think of?

_____

_____

_____

_____

_____

3. When we get angry, what could we perhaps do to avoid lashing out at others?

_____

_____

_____

_____

_____

_____

4. How can we get angry but not sin against God?

_____

_____

_____

_____

_____

5. When choosing a name for their child, what kind of things might parents consider?

_____

_____

_____

_____

_____

6. What do you think is our spiritual birthright?

_____

_____

_____

_____

_____

7. How might we be robbed of our spiritual birthright?

_____

_____

_____

_____

_____

8. How has God redeemed some of your mistakes in the past?

_____

_____

_____

_____

_____

Personal Application

When we receive a promise from God, we might think that for it to happen we need to interfere or help God out by doing things our own way (especially if we aren't prepared to wait!). One example of this is Jacob's grandfather Abraham, who decided to take matters into his own hands and start a family via his servant girl Hagar, rather than waiting for God's promise to be fulfilled in his wife, Sarah.

Jacob was eager for spiritual blessings, but the way in which he sought to obtain them was not pleasing to God. Lies and deceit may come naturally to us; as flawed human beings, dishonesty is part of our sinful nature. Seeking God in prayer is important so that we are more spiritually prepared to act honestly and with integrity, and trust His perfect will.

The Bible describes Satan as a 'liar', and the 'father of lies' (John 8:44). Every word he speaks is a lie; there is no truth in him. As God's people, let's not believe anything Satan says. Let's choose to believe God's best for us and endeavour to live more like Jesus.

Seeing Jesus in the Scriptures

When Jesus was on earth, He constantly found himself in potentially awkward or difficult situations, but He always responded in a righteous way, and by doing so He always pleased His Father. A great example of this can be found in Luke 20:20–26, where spies were sent to trap Jesus in His words. But Jesus 'saw through their duplicity' (v23) and responded with truth and integrity. Because He answered them so wisely, the spies were so astonished that it shut them up!

WEEK THREE

Jacob's dream

Opening Icebreaker

Name some people in Scripture who met with God face to face. What were their experiences? How were they changed afterwards?

Bible Readings

- Genesis 27:42–44; 28:1–5,10–22
- Deuteronomy 31:8
- Jeremiah 17:7–8

Key verse: 'I am with you and will watch over you wherever you go, and I will bring you back to this land. I will not leave you until I have done what I have promised you.' (Gen. 28:15)

Focus: God longs to meet with us. He is with us in all our troubles.

Opening Our Eyes

At his mother's instruction, Jacob fled to his uncle Laban's home until Esau could perhaps one day forgive him. Isaac sent Jacob on his way with his blessing, so he left his home in Beersheba and travelled to another country – Harran – somewhere he had never been.

As a stranger in a foreign land, Jacob probably would have felt lonely and afraid. He was by himself, going somewhere totally unfamiliar. But fortunately, he knew about God and he believed that He would help him in his plight. He knew about the God of his grandfather Abraham, his father Isaac, and he also knew about the promises that God had already spoken over his life.

When Jacob became weary, he slept – and God gave him a divine dream. He spoke to Jacob telling him what He would do, and reaffirmed the promise that was given to him. Jacob had a glimpse of heaven and was reassured that his God was with him on this journey to Laban's household.

God reassures us, too, giving us words of encouragement to help us on our way. He might speak through prayer, His Word, a song, other people or preaching, but He is always speaking to His children; we just need to listen to His voice. There have been many times in my own life when all seemed lost and I felt spiritually weak. But then God would speak to me through some avenue – a word of encouragement – which would lift me up in my spirit so that I was refreshed. How about you?

When Jacob awoke, he knew that he'd had an encounter with God, and he made a pillar to mark the place. This is something people in Bible times did; they would make a physical reference point to remember when, where and how God had met with them. Jacob set up his pillar from the rock he had laid his head on as he slept, and named the place Bethel, which means 'house of God'.

As Christians, it's easy to forget that God has spoken to us, so it's important for us to have some reference points of our own. This doesn't have to be anything as major as building a tower, but it's worth considering how we can landmark God's goodness in our lives. With 'milestone' encounters, we can look back at our map of blessings in tough times and be encouraged that God has everything under control. Nothing takes God by surprise – He goes before us (Deut. 31:8), and knows what's coming.

In response to his life-changing encounter with God, Jacob made a vow, promising that if God provided for him and protected him, then he would serve Him. This is a pivotal moment in Jacob's journey of character. When we choose to serve God, He begins to change us slowly to make us more like Him. He is the potter, and we are the clay in His hands (Jer. 18:6). He knows what He is doing – all we have to do is trust and obey Him, and He will do the rest (see Jer. 17:7–8).

Jacob's journey had been rather eventful, but another life-changing encounter awaited him at his uncle's house: he was about to meet Rachel.

Discussion Starters

1. Think of a couple of people in the Bible who fled
something, somewhere or someone. What happened?

_____

_____

_____

_____

_____

2. Can you think of a journey you've been on in life
(physical, spiritual or emotional) where you've really
felt that God was with you?

_____

_____

_____

_____

_____

3. How has God spoken to you in the past?

_____

_____

_____

_____

_____

4. How could we make physical reference points of our
own so that we don't forget times when God has met
with us?

_____

_____

_____

_____

_____

5. What promises has God made to you? What promises (if any) have you made to God?

_____

_____

_____

_____

_____

6. How can having a grateful heart transform our relationship with God?

_____

_____

_____

_____

_____

7. Our God is Jehovah Jireh – God who provides. In what ways does God provide for those who trust in Him?

_____

_____

_____

_____

_____

8. What are some of the blessings we receive from God just by being His children?

_____

_____

_____

_____

_____

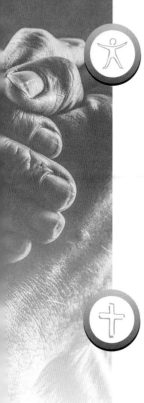

Personal Application

When God clearly spoke to Jacob, it changed his life forever. He responded in the right way – by worshipping God, marking the experience with a monument, and making a vow, which he kept. It's the same for us and for everyone who meets with God – we are changed forever.

So how do we respond? Making time to praise God in our busy lives is essential. Worship is necessary as God is worthy and He calls us to praise and worship Him. But praise is also powerful; it takes our mind off all our troubles so that we can fix our eyes on Jesus and focus on Him.

Seeing Jesus in the Scriptures

God met Jacob right where he was, to give him encouragement and reappoint him for His purposes. Similarly, Jesus is constantly encouraging us on our way. He is only a breath away – a prayer away – and He will meet with us to bring reassurance and hope. We only need to ask Him.

Jesus Himself was encouraged and strengthened several times during His ministry, such as after He had been tempted by the devil (see Matt. 4:1–11). He understands what we are going through, and He loves to build up and strengthen His people.

WEEK FOUR

Jacob – husband and father

Icebreaker

Get some index cards and write the names of Jacob's children on them, one name on each card. Then get your group to lay them out in order of their birth (the answer is in the Leader's Notes). If there are lots of you, why not try this in two teams?

Bible Readings

- Genesis 29; 30:17–24
- Proverbs 29:17; 22:6
- Psalm 37:4

Key verse: 'Jacob was in love with Rachel and said, "I'll work for you seven years in return for your younger daughter Rachel."' (Gen. 29:18)

Focus: God knows the desires of our hearts, so we can trust Him with our lives.

Opening Our Eyes

It was love at first sight! We can just picture it: Jacob claps eyes on the lovely Rachel and is instantly compelled to know her. He shows off his strength by moving a heavy rock and helping her with her shepherding duties (Gen. 29:10). And before you know it, he kisses her. He's moved to tears and instantly they become the best of friends.

Jacob was accepted into Laban's family, and went to work on his lands. But, as another romantic gesture, Jacob wants no wages for his labour – only Rachel's hand in marriage.

Can you imagine being given the opportunity to choose your own salary and deciding to work unpaid? Jacob had no possessions or money and in those days the bride had to be 'paid for', so to speak, so Jacob offered what he could – his time and labour – and shepherded Laban's flocks. He was so in love with Rachel that those seven years felt like mere days (Gen. 29:20).

Seven years is a long time to keep your hands off the love of your life! But perhaps we could take a leaf out of Jacob's book. Our culture is impatient for whatever it desires. Many consider it to be normal and right to be able to sleep with whoever they like, whenever they like. Teenagers are often somehow ashamed of their virginity. However, as Christians, God requires something different from us when it comes to our sexual purity, and He always has. We are called to live counter-culturally by placing a higher value on sex, and that applies to all of us, whether married or single (see 1 Cor. 6:12–20). And Jacob honoured God by waiting for his wife – even though God had not yet given the Ten Commandments.

Perhaps this is what makes the next part of the story all the more difficult for Jacob, although we might view it as somewhat poetic: the deceiver became the deceived.

Jacob's wedding night was not what he hoped it would be; he ended up consummating his marriage not with Rachel, but with Leah, her older sister. Just imagine how Jacob felt! It might seem unbelievable, but through a likely combination of a veiled bride and a lot of darkness, Jacob had been utterly deceived.

And so, for a further seven years of hard labour, Jacob had two wives – and they were sisters, at that! It must have been awkward. Imagine the conflicts that may have arisen within their home. Jacob hadn't wanted Leah, and that would likely have caused her much pain. He probably cared for her, but it was Rachel whom he loved.

It's interesting to note that although Leah had borne Jacob a daughter and six sons (half of the twelve tribes of Israel), he still favoured Rachel and her fewer children. Remember that favouritism had been the cause of rifts in Isaac and Rebekah's household? Well, Jacob didn't do a great job of breaking the cycle, and found his favourite in Joseph, for whom he made a coat of many colours (see Gen. 37). The rest of his sons were constantly opposed to each other, and there were frequent contentions fuelled by anger, jealousy and revenge. The chain reaction of Laban's wedding deception was further division and tension that would go down in history.

?? Discussion Starters

1. Why is sexual purity important to God?

_____
_____
_____
_____
_____
_____

2. Why do you think Jesus taught that a man should have only one wife? (See Matt. 19:1–9.)

_____
_____
_____
_____
_____

3. Consider some biblical examples of married couples. How did God use them?

_____
_____
_____
_____
_____
_____

4. Why is it important for Christian parents to teach their children about God?

_____
_____
_____
_____
_____

5. How might Jacob's favouritism of Rachel's children have affected the family dynamic?

_____

_____

_____

_____

_____

6. Discuss some ways in which we can model Christian living to the children we know and love.

_____

_____

_____

_____

_____

_____

7. How could you invite God into your own family life?

_____

_____

_____

_____

_____

_____

8. What could help us as we wait for our heart's desires to be fulfilled?

_____

_____

_____

_____

_____

_____

Personal Application

There are so many lessons about family life that we can learn from Jacob – from how we conduct ourselves when we are single or dating, to how we love our spouse and any children.

When choosing someone to be your spouse, their character (and yours!) is what's most important. Prayer is an essential part of this process too and it's vital that God is involved in your decision making.

If you are single and desire to be married one day, keep on pressing in to God and praying for whoever that person might be. Just wait and trust in God to bring about His purposes in your life at the right time.

Seeing Jesus in the Scriptures

Despite the domestic turbulence in Jacob's family household, this story has a redemptive thread. Generations later, Jesus was born into the line of Judah. It's amazing that God should choose such a messy family legacy to be born into Himself – let alone the bloodline of Judah, who betrayed his own brother (Joseph, Jacob's favourite son) and sold him into slavery. In fact, the story of Joseph holds many parallels with the life of Jesus (some commentators think there are as many as 100 prophetic similarities between the two). And all this from the house of Jacob… what a legacy!

WEEK FIVE

Jacob leaves blessed

Icebreaker

Have there been times in your life when God blessed you abundantly? What happened?

Bible Readings

- Genesis 30:25–43; 31:1–9,17–21
- Ephesians 3:20

Key verse: 'In this way the man [Jacob] grew exceedingly prosperous and came to own large flocks, and female and male servants, and camels and donkeys.' (Gen. 30:43)

Focus: God blesses His people when they are faithful to obey Him.

Opening Our Eyes

As we consider Jacob's family life, it's easy to see that God was with him. Jacob had 13 children (12 sons and a daughter), four wives, and he worked hard to provide for his family. Even Uncle Laban, who didn't actually believe in God, realised that Jacob was blessed because he was staying on his land (which is why he was desperate for Jacob to remain with him!). When people are blessed by God it is obvious, and everyone wants to be around blessed people!

Jacob agreed to stay with Laban for a while longer until he could obtain some livestock of his own and provide for his family. Through rather unorthodox farming methods, we see Jacob deliberately breed strong, speckled livestock. It could be that God gave Jacob a divine strategy for producing such strong animals, or it could be that He blessed Jacob's plans regardless of his methods. Either way, Jacob knows that it is God who has increased his flock (Gen. 31:9).

God shows us what steps to take when we ask Him, and He blesses us abundantly. We all face times of struggle and difficulty, but even during these times our Father provides for His children because He loves us and He always has our best interests at heart.

Although God told Jacob to leave and go back to his homeland, we see Jacob's deceiving tendencies resurface once again. Rather than face Laban, he fled, perhaps out of fear. From what we read, it sounds like he also left in this way out of a right to take whatever he wanted, rather than trust God to provide for him. So, he deceived once again – he took his family and left. When we allow fear or a sense of entitlement to cloud our judgment, it can take hold of us and cause us to make rash decisions.

Although Jacob was obeying God's instructions to leave, he didn't go about it in the right way.

Rachel, too, acted dishonestly by stealing Laban's household idols. Perhaps she wanted to hold on to her past and the old way of doing things, or she might have wanted to hurt her father by taking something that was precious to him. But she too, like her husband, exercised deceit. (Many Bible scholars think that the household idols got passed to the heir of the family and whoever had them was entitled to the family inheritance, which is perhaps why Laban was so intent on getting them back.) It is interesting to consider that Jacob was assisted in his deception of Esau by his mother, Rebekah, and later in his deception of Laban by his wife.

But once again, God intervened on Jacob's behalf by appearing to Laban in a dream, warning him not to harm Jacob. Jacob tried to run away from his problems (notice a pattern here?) but facing them would have been the best cause of action. God always intended for Jacob to be protected and blessed by Him. He is our Father, and we are His children. He loves to bless us and meet our needs, just as an earthly father should. And, by the grace of God – despite all the tensions, deceptions and disagreements – Jacob and Laban were eventually able to part ways agreeably.

Discussion Starters

1. Have you, like Jacob, ever acted out of fear or a sense of entitlement and found yourself in unnecessary trouble?

   _____

   _____

   _____

   _____

   _____

   _____

2. Why do you think we, as humans, let our own perspectives eclipse what God is telling us?

   _____

   _____

   _____

   _____

   _____

3. God is a blesser! Why may giving back to God financially be good for us?

   _____

   _____

   _____

   _____

   _____

4. What are some of the things you would consider to be idols in our modern world?

   _____

   _____

   _____

   _____

   _____

5. Why do you think God hates idols?

_____

_____

_____

_____

_____

_____

6. How can we avoid being influenced by others to deceive? How can we encourage others to value integrity?

_____

_____

_____

_____

_____

7. How has God blessed you? Why may it help to remind ourselves of His blessings?

_____

_____

_____

_____

_____

8. What could we do to ensure we are putting God first in our lives?

_____

_____

_____

_____

_____

Personal Application

As God's children, we too, like Rachel, can find ourselves carrying idols with us. An idol doesn't have to be a physical thing – it could be something inside our heads – anything that we love more than God, or something we would rather do than be with Him. Do you feel the Lord prompting you about any such areas of your life that you could realign according to His priorities?

Jacob's attitude in these passages shows us a lot about the human condition. Even when God wants us to move forward in something, we can easily let our own ideas and agendas get in the way of God's best for us. Sometimes it is fear, greed or our taking offence that trips us up. Let's not allow personal disagreements to go unresolved or drag on for years. Allow God to challenge you on any such quarrels that might be ongoing within your own family, friendship group or workplace.

Seeing Jesus in the Scriptures

God is so good to us that sometimes we forget what He has saved us from. Jesus paid the price of our sin to set us free and save us from death. God has blessed us much more than we deserve! We are sinners, saved by God's grace, and we would have been bound to an eternity without Him were it not for God's unwavering love for us. Why not make it a daily habit to spend some time reflecting on what Jesus has done for you?

WEEK SIX

Jacob wrestles with God

Opening Icebreaker

If you were a professional wrestler, what would your stage name be?

Bible Readings

- Genesis 32:3–12,22–30; 33:1–11
- Luke 18:1–8
- Matthew 7:7–11

Key verse: 'Then the man said, "Let me go, for it is daybreak." But Jacob replied, "I will not let you go unless you bless me."' (Gen. 32:26)

Focus: Prevailing in prayer.

Opening Our Eyes

Having reconciled with Laban, Jacob continued on his journey home, but had yet to patch things up with his brother, Esau. It must have taken a lot of faith just to send word that he was on his way back home, so imagine his fear when his messengers came back telling him that his brother was on his way with 400 men! Did Jacob think his time was up? He cried out to God to help him again. Finally, we see Jacob as a truly transformed man: he became a man of faith instead of a man of fear.

Then we read that a man, who seemed to appear from nowhere, wrestled with Jacob throughout the night. This man we know to be God incarnate, as Jacob declares: 'I saw God face to face, and yet my life was spared' (Gen. 32:30). It's interesting to read that the man 'could not overpower' Jacob, such was his persistence in the struggle.

It is the same for us when we persevere in prayer. So often we can give up on prayer, perhaps believing that God simply will not answer certain prayers, especially if we have been praying for a long time without seeing any physical results. But persevering in prayer is how breakthrough comes. Consider the case of the widow and the judge in Luke 18:1–8. She sought justice, but had to be persistent in her request until she was satisfied. Unlike the unjust judge, God is not exhausted by our nagging, and doesn't give in to our requests to get rid of us. By persisting in prayer, our faith is both stretched and strengthened. Some things can only be received from God when we persist in our prayers. And we can be confident that God hears us (Matt. 7:7–11) – so let's have the confidence to ask Him for blessing!

As Jacob clung to God, he said that he wouldn't let go unless God blessed him. This may sound like a bold request, but our God loves an audacious prayer. If Jacob hadn't asked then he possibly wouldn't have received, but God gave him what he asked for.

From that day on, Jacob was called Israel, meaning 'struggles with God'. By dislocating Jacob's hip, God left him with a permanent reminder of the time they had wrestled. We can often be swift to forget our encounters with God. Having been touched by God in this way, Jacob walked with a limp – a picture of how he would have to lean and rely on God from that point onwards.

When Jacob meets his brother Esau again, their reunion is almost like that of the prodigal son: 'Esau ran to meet Jacob and embraced him; he threw his arms around his neck and kissed him. And they wept' (Gen. 22:4). They had not met since Jacob received his father's blessing deceitfully. What a beautiful picture this is of God's grace, and His heart that we be reconciled to each other.

Forgiveness is a powerful weapon. It can be difficult to forgive people who have hurt us – and often, it isn't something we can do in our own strength. But when we have the Holy Spirit living inside us, anything is possible. God helps us to forgive as He forgave us. It doesn't mean that the other person was right, it just means that we are right with God. We can release our bitterness, anger and hatred into God's hands. Justice belongs to Him.

Discussion Starters

1. As believers, why is prayer so important in our lives?

2. What might our prayers consist of? Is there a prayer pattern that we should follow?

3. Do you sometimes pray 'toned down' versions of your prayers so that you don't appear 'too bold'? Why?

4. Do you find that praying can be a real struggle sometimes? Why do you think that is?

5. Do you think God still would have blessed Jacob, even if Jacob hadn't asked Him to?

_____

_____

_____

_____

_____

_____

6. Do you have any stories of reconciliation?

_____

_____

_____

_____

_____

7. Is there something you are 'wrestling with God' for at the moment?

_____

_____

_____

_____

_____

_____

8. Why do you think Esau forgave Jacob after all those years?

_____

_____

_____

_____

_____

_____

Personal Application

Prayer is vital for us as believers, and it's important for us to set aside time every day for personal prayer. For Jacob, prayer was an interactive, two-way conversation; it was honest and real.

As well as prayer, it's good to set aside a few moments for personal meditation – not so much 'wrestling' as listening, reading and thinking about God's Word. Reading the Bible is how we grow in our knowledge of God and our understanding of His character. Even if you can only manage to read a few verses each day, you will be amazed at what God will show you.

Seeing Jesus in the Scriptures

Even Jesus – who *is* God – prayed when He was on earth. We see some amazing examples of His prayers in the Bible, such as the Lord's Prayer (Matt. 6:9–13) and the High Priestly Prayer (John 17). Jesus was in constant communication with His Father, sometimes even praying through the night. Have you ever prayed all night for something?

In a way, Jesus also wrestled with God when He prayed in the Garden of Gethsemane just before His arrest. A key passage where we see Jesus' humanity and divinity in conflict is Matthew 26:36–46. We read that He asked 'for this cup to be taken away' no fewer than three times.

We can follow Jesus' example of honest, heartfelt prayer. We can petition God from our deepest places of anxiety, pain or longing. He strengthens us for what is to come.

WEEK SEVEN

Jacob returns to his homeland

Icebreaker

What's the most amazing place you have ever travelled to? How do you feel when you return home after a long time away?

Bible Readings

- Genesis 35
- Psalm 119:105
- Matthew 6:25–34
- Jeremiah 29:11–13

Key verse: 'Then God said to Jacob, "Go up to Bethel and settle there, and build an altar there to God, who appeared to you when you were fleeing from your brother Esau."' (Gen. 35:1)

Focus: God directs our steps and shows us where we should go.

Opening Our Eyes

Remember the Jacob who ran away from home after deceiving his father and dividing his family? Well, many years, four wives and 13 children later, we see him go full circle and make the journey home. As the first stop along the way, God directs Jacob to the place where they had their first encounter.

Throughout these studies we have seen that, time and time again, God met with Jacob and directed his steps, despite Jacob repeatedly insisting on trying things his own way. What an encouragement for us!

Jacob was not perfect – nobody is – but God still loved him and met his every need, and the same is true for us today. His Word is a lamp for our feet and a guide to our path (Psa. 119:105).

Jacob ran away at various points in his life. He fled from his brother Esau, then he fled from Uncle Laban. Despite the plans that God had for Jacob, Jacob chose to try things his own way first – and still, God made a way to bring him back to his homeland.

All of us have gone our own way. The world is broken, and sin has separated us from God. But He has made it His mission to bring us home. Jesus made a way for us to be with Him forever, by dying on the cross for our sins so that we can make heaven our home. This was always God's plan for mankind – this is our true home.

Jacob's journey home was not an easy one. 'While they were still some distance' from home (Gen. 35:16), he had to see Rachel, the wife he loved, suffer through a difficult childbirth that ended up claiming her life. But he was able to take his twelfth son, Benjamin, with him in returning to their homeland. In our own journeys towards our heavenly home, it is likely that not everyone who travels with us will always be there, but there will be others who join us as we walk.

Let's remind ourselves of what transformed Jacob into a man of God in the first place: a life-changing encounter with Him. From that day on, God always spoke to Jacob and gave him direction and hope. The blessings poured into his life.

In Genesis 35:9, we see another such encounter: 'God appeared to him again and blessed him.' Do you remember discussing the importance of the meanings of names in an earlier study? Here, God removes the 'deceiver' from Jacob's identity, and replaces it with a new name, 'Israel', or 'he struggles with God'. Jacob moved from being a liar to a real and honest pray-er who could depend on the God he loved. To this day, his descendants make up the nation that still wrestle with God for His promises.

When God comes near, and pours out His blessings on us, we are changed. We are given a new identity, and a new home. If we could only realise how much God loves and cares for us, then we wouldn't just settle for the mediocre of life but contend for greater things. God desires to bless us abundantly, if only we would ask Him.

Jacob wasn't about to simply settle in to a comfortable retirement once he arrived home. Indeed, he had yet to bury his father, and later face the trial of the temporary loss of his favourite son, Joseph (Gen. 37). But God's hand was upon him and his family for the rest of their lives, for generations to come.

Discussion Starters

1. Making a new start with God is always possible – why is that?

   _____
   _____
   _____
   _____
   _____
   _____

2. Think of some people in the Bible whose steps were directed by God, even if it meant going in the opposite direction to the one they were planning! What did they learn?

   _____
   _____
   _____
   _____
   _____
   _____

3. Why do you think God sent Jacob back to the place of their first encounter?

   _____
   _____
   _____
   _____
   _____
   _____

4. As Christians, how can we wisely plan for our future?

   _____
   _____
   _____
   _____
   _____

5. What does Matthew 6:25–34 teach us about our future?

_____

_____

_____

_____

_____

_____

6. How will trusting God with our future help us?

_____

_____

_____

_____

_____

7. How can we be encouraged by Jeremiah 29:11–13?

_____

_____

_____

_____

_____

8. In your opinion, what was Jacob's greatest blessing from God?

_____

_____

_____

_____

_____

Personal Application

In the account of their journey home in Genesis 35, God told Jacob to get rid of all the household gods in order for them to be cleansed and for God to be able to bless them. God hates idolatry, and wants us to stay away from anything that distracts us from Him. He doesn't want us to pick up things that are no good for us. Take some time to consider what you might have picked up along your journey that might be hindering your walk with God. These aren't always 'things'; they can be negative attitudes, unforgiveness and hatred. What could you choose to leave behind today?

Seeing Jesus in the Scriptures

Jesus was the bridge to make a way for us to come 'home' to God. We are reconciled back to the Father because of Jesus' sacrifice. He took our sins and nailed them to the cross so that we may be forgiven and we can make heaven our home – not by doing good works, and not that we deserve it, but because God loves us so much that He wants us to be with Him forever. Like Jacob, we have wandered off, but Jesus is our route home.

If you want to start a homeward journey towards Jesus today, here is a simple prayer:

Lord Jesus, I'm sorry for going my own way. Please forgive me for everything I have done wrong. I believe that You came to earth to die for me and bring me back home to You. I believe that You are alive today, and with me every moment. Come into my heart and make me new so that I can live for You. Amen.

Leader's Notes

Week One: Jacob's beginning

General Thoughts

A key theme to bring through this study is God's plan. Isaac and Rebekah had a relationship with God and knew what He could do in their lives, which made them persevere in their prayers for children. They had to wait many years but God made it happen. Rebekah gave birth to twin boys and these boys would change the course of history.

Discussion Starters

It is worth considering that the issue of childlessness may be difficult for some people in your group, so be sensitive to how discussion on this issue develops. If you know that this is the case for people attending your study, be clear that although God doesn't answer all prayers in the same way, He is still good, and has a plan. Make sure people feel encouraged, not the opposite. Do your best to ensure that discussion around family – particularly sibling rivalry or parenting – stays positive and constructive.

Helpful Bible Verses

Throughout Scripture, we see that God is faithful to His people. He is always waiting to spend time with us and He loves to not only hear but answer our prayers. Over the page are a few scriptures about God being faithful to encourage your group with:

- Hebrews 10:23
- 2 Thessalonians 3:3
- Deuteronomy 7:9
- 1 Corinthians 1:9

Prayer

Isaac and Rebekah were blessed by God, but they had to wait a long time and persist in prayer for many years. There will likely be people in your group who can relate to this, and they may or may not feel comfortable sharing. Doubt and discouragement are very normal things to experience, but through waiting, God works in our character and begins to change us and make us more and more like Jesus. He is patient with us and works with us to help us grow both physically and spiritually. Encourage your group to continue to wait on the Lord as He will come through for them in the end.

Why not make time at the end of the study to recommit some of your long-term requests to God?

Week Two: Jacob the deceiver

General Thoughts

The aim of this study is to encourage your group to act in ways that will please God, focusing on being righteous (doing the right thing) and not lashing out in anger or sin.

It's important to remember that anger is an emotion. We might think that all anger is wrong, but God shows us that anger can be either righteous or unrighteous. A righteous anger is the kind that Jesus had when He went into the Temple to find people selling goods in it, rather than praying and seeking the Lord. He was very rightly angry at what He saw and so He drove out the animals on sale and overturned the tables (John 2:13–17).

Unrighteous anger, however, is the kind that we need to stay clear of; this is the kind of anger that Esau displayed in our text.

Here are some ways to counteract this kind of anger, that you may wish to suggest to your group:

- Pray – forgive those that have hurt us and ask Jesus to help us to check our emotions.
- Give our problems to the Lord and ask for grace to not get angry with people who might interfere.
- Count to ten – a great way to counteract anger and a good thing to do before replying to someone who has made you angry.
- Fix your eyes on Jesus – stop focusing on the problem and give God praise for what He is about to do in your life. Then God fills us with His peace and calms us down.
- Remember – anger is an emotion that isn't always based on reality, so try to think of some relaxing

thoughts instead. Try to see the humorous side of it too – this may help you to feel back in control.

To keep discussion positive, try to focus on our spiritual birthright and what Christ has achieved for us on the cross, and how any mistake we make can be redeemed by God.

Discussion Starters

2. Some examples you could offer:

- Abraham lying and saying that Sarah was his sister, not his wife (Gen. 20:2).
- Joseph's brothers tearing his tunic and dipping it in animal blood to deceive Jacob (Gen. 37:31).
- Herod trying to deceive the Magi (Matt. 2:8).

8. When sharing personal experiences, be careful to avoid giving 'too much information' with regard to talking about other people. Focus on the redemption more than the mistake.

Helpful Bible Verses

- Ephesians 1:18–19
- Galations 3:29
- Isaiah 1:18

Prayer

When discussing the issue of deception, some individuals may feel tempted to bring up past hurts. Avoid specifics, and try to keep discussion positive – if appropriate, consider offering prayer after the session or at a more private time.

Week Three: Jacob's dream

General Thoughts

A key theme for this week is encountering God. You can probably expect varying degrees of experience of this among your group, and if you have time, you could consider inviting people to share some of their encounters with God. Before you begin your session, have a think about what your own experiences have been, and how God has changed you as a result.

Another thing to consider, thematically, is praise and worship. Do we give God thanks and praise?

Encourage your group to praise God even through times of hardship and difficulty. God loves to hear our praises. We were created to praise Him, and this is even more important when we go through difficult times, as God pays close attention to how we respond to Him in these times of trial. Worship is something that comes out of our lives when we live a life that pleases God.

Discussion Starters

1. You might consider the following examples:

- David fleeing various enemies throughout 1 Samuel and the book of Psalms.
- Elijah running from Jezebel.
- Jonah going in the opposite direction to Nineveh.
- Mary and Joseph, with baby Jesus, who fled from the terror of Herod.
- Jesus' disciples who went into hiding after He was crucified.

4. Jacob set up a pillar in our text. This was a literal stone that people put up so they would remember

the place where they had an encounter with God. It was a sign of remembrance as we tend to forget things easily. Obviously we don't set up physical pillars in our modern world, but it's important to record special times when God has met with us – not only so that we remember, but so that we can look at them in times of difficulty and be encouraged.

5.　God takes vows extremely seriously, so we need to be clear about why we would be making one in the first place. Focus on the positive aspects of making a covenant with God, and do your best to ensure that no one feels under pressure to make a vow.

Helpful Bible Verses

- Numbers 30:2
- Deuteronomy 23:21–23
- Ecclesiastes 5:4–5

Prayer

Some members of your group may seek prayer support in keeping promises that they have made to God. Consider how you might support and uphold the godly promises that those in your group might have made.

Week Four: Jacob – husband and father

General Thoughts

Group discussions about sex, marriage and raising children can be a minefield, but make space for people to discuss these things. As a group leader, be careful not to be judgmental of other people's experiences, and remember that God places a tremendous amount of value on marriage and sex.

Icebreaker

Jacob's children in order of birth are: Reuben, Simeon, Levi, Judah, Dan, Naphtali, Gad, Asher, Issachar, Zebulun, Dinah, Joseph, Benjamin.

Discussion Starters

1. See above. If you know in advance that there are opposing views on this within your group, consider what your church's standpoint is on sex and marriage. Try not to let the entire session revolve around this issue, however, as the main focus is on Jacob's family specifically.

3. Some examples you might consider:

- Adam and Eve.
- Boaz and Ruth.
- Hosea and Gomer.
- Abraham and Sarah.
- Mary and Joseph.

5. Discussion around favouritism and sibling rivalry can be tricky, so take care to keep things positive. If this is an issue that members of your group are struggling with, make sure you know what support is available in your church.

6. Within your group you might have parents, grandparents, godparents, aunts, uncles, teachers, nurses, childminders... most of us will have children in our lives. Encourage your group to inspire the children in your church to seek the Lord and serve Him, as you all do. Consider how to make Christianity exciting for them, and teach them how to pray and read the Bible.

(Samuel was given to the Lord from birth – and look how he turned out!)

Helpful Bible Verses

For discussing sexual purity:
- 1 Corinthians 6:15–20
- Romans 12:1–2
- Ephesians 5:3

For discussing parenting:
- Proverbs 22:6
- Deuteronomy 6:6–7
- Ephesians 6:4

Prayer

You might consider praying for each other within your group – whether single, married, divorced, bereaved, parents, or longing to have children. Don't press each other for details, and respect privacy, but pray that God would give you the desires of your heart, and that you would honour Him in your relationships and family life.

Pray also for school (and Sunday school) teachers, who invest in the lives of the children you all know. Seek God in how we can better model His love to the younger generation.

Week Five: Jacob leaves blessed

General Thoughts

We can all be hugely distracted by both fear and a sense of entitlement, as Jacob was. During your discussion time, it's possible that people in your group may open up about things causing them worry, stress or anxiety, or perhaps they are feeling resentful about something they think is owed to them or overdue. If such things are covered by your discussion, they can be great opportunities for prayer later on. Also, see some useful Bible verses about this below.

The focus of this book is 'taking hold of God's blessing'. Consider – are there things people in your group might be wanting to step into? In what areas of their lives do they want to see breakthrough?

God loves to bless His people in all manner of ways, and there is nothing wrong with having money and nice things. It is because of God's nature as a giver and a loving Father that He desires to bless His people not just a little, but abundantly. We may go through seasons of financial difficulty, but as we persist in prayer, God will come through for us. Encourage your group to contend for God's blessings in their daily lives – not for 'prosperity', but for God's goodness.

Discussion Starters

3. When discussing finances (particularly giving/tithing), be aware of the varying degrees of wealth in your group. Nothing is wasted in God's economy – indeed, His resources are infinite, and He always multiplies and blesses. Encourage your group to live generously, but be sensitive of financial pressures and avoid specifying figures.

8. Something you might consider suggesting is accountability groups (smaller 'small groups' within the one you are meeting in for this study, of two to three people maximum). They provide a great environment for friendships to develop, people to share their struggles honestly, and for people to challenge and encourage one another to put God first!

Helpful Bible Verses:

- Joshua 1:9
- Romans 8:28
- John 16:33
- Deuteronomy 31:8

Prayer

Consider any points that might have been raised in your earlier discussions.

Week Six: Jacob wrestles with God

General Thoughts

As Christians it's vital to have a regular daily prayer life with God. We cannot be spiritually strong if we do not pray and therefore become easy targets for the enemy to attack. Jesus is our perfect example of someone who had a regular prayer life, and if Jesus (who *is* God) prayed, then we definitely need to!

Our lives can be so hectic, and in a culture of the immediate, it can be particularly difficult to set aside time. Encourage your group to make prayer a priority in their lives, and to 'wrestle' with God for healing, provision, reconciliation etc.

Discussion Starters

2. If you have some new Christians in your group, discussion here might be really beneficial. As a basic guide, you might consider the 'teaspoon' model, or TSP: Thank You, Sorry, Please. Our prayers should cover thanksgiving, repentance, and petitioning God with our requests and desires.

4-7. Spiritual warfare is real, and something we can expect to face when we are pursuing God's best for us. Persistence in prayer is so important. The story of the woman and the unjust judge (Luke 18:1–8) encourages us to persist in asking God until breakthrough comes. It's easy to give up when we do not see instant results. But God loves us to press in, to contend, and just like Jacob, to grab hold of Him and not let go until He answers our prayers.

There are many reasons why God might not answer us immediately. He might be using circumstances to draw us closer to Him, test our faith, test our patience, test our motives, improve our character etc. All we can do is keep persisting and trust in God's purposes, waiting by faith for Him to move for us.

Helpful Bible Verses

- Ephesians 6:18
- 1 Peter 5:7
- Philippians 4:6–7
- Luke 18:1

Prayer

Pray for breakthrough!

If anyone has shared what they are 'wrestling' with God for, lift them up in prayer. Encourage this to go on even after your group study has finished. If people have shared stories of breakthrough they've seen as a result of 'wrestling', consider reminding each other of these as you pray.

Week Seven: Jacob returns to his homeland

General Thoughts

As our study draws to a close, use this session to recap what you have learned from Jacob's journey through life. God redeemed his mistakes, guided his steps, and brought Jacob home to where he belonged. If you have anyone in your group who has not yet made a commitment to following Jesus, you may wish to gently suggest this (without applying any pressure).

Other Christians in the group may wish to reflect upon their own journeys with God.

Ultimately, this session is about trusting God with our future, pursuing His plans for our lives, and recommitting ourselves to following Him.

Discussion Starters

2. There are endless examples in the Bible, but if people are struggling with ideas, you could consider suggesting Abraham, Isaac, Ruth and Naomi, Elijah, Esther, David, Jonah, John the Baptist, Paul etc.

4. Remember that it is important to trust God with our future, as only He knows what is ahead, but we are also called to be good stewards and be wise with our finances. Everything belongs to God – our money, our clothes, our children, everything. God owns all the wealth of this world and He has no problems in blessing us as His children. If there are people struggling financially in your group, direct them towards sound, Christian financial advice (CAP – Christians Against Poverty – is a great place to start).

5-6. The Bible tells us repeatedly not to worry! (See some Bible verses below.) When we worry, we are not focusing on God, and that means the enemy has us right where he wants us! You may wish to use the suggested list of scriptures as a starting point for combatting worry.

Helpful Bible Verses

For discussing 'homecoming':
- 1 Peter 2:9–10
- Ephesians 1:3–14
- John 3:16

For discussing worry:
- Philippians 4:8
- Matthew 6:25–27
- Luke 12:29

For discussing finances:
- Malachi 3:8–12
- Proverbs 11:25
- Proverbs 3:9
- Hebrews 13:5

Prayer

As this session concludes the study, give thanks for what you have learned. Consider what points each of you would like to take forward and continue developing in your walk with the Lord.

If anyone prayed the prayer of repentance at the end of this study, be sure to follow up with them!

Here are a few scriptures that might help them:

- Luke 15:10
- 2 Corinthians 5:17
- 1 Corinthians 10:13
- 1 Peter 5:7
- 1 John 1:9

Notes...

Be inspired by God.
Every day.

EVERY DAY
MAY/JUN 2017

Isaiah 40-66
2 Peter & Jude

Bringing you deeper biblical understanding **CWR**

One-year subscriptions available for all titles

Cover to Cover Every Day

In-depth study of the Bible, book by book. Part of a five-year series. Available as an email subscription or on eBook and Kindle.

Every Day with Jesus

The popular daily Bible reading notes by Selwyn Hughes.

Inspiring Women Every Day

Daily insight and encouragement written by women for women.

Life Every Day

Lively Bible notes, with Jeff Lucas' wit and wisdom.

To order or subscribe, visit **www.cwr.org.uk/store** or call **01252 784700**.
Also available in Christian bookshops.

 Print subscription available

 **Large Print subscription** available

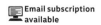 **Email subscription** available

Latest Resource

Haggai - Motivating God's People
by Steve Bishop

Haggai, a perhaps overlooked prophet, was all about motivating God's people into action. He reminded the Israelites of how God had greatly blessed them, and encouraged them to live for His purposes. Join Steve Bishop as he gets to the heart of this book and discover how it still applies to us today.

72-page booklet, 210x148mm
ISBN: 978-1-78259-686-8

The Popular *Cover to Cover* Bible Study Series

1 Corinthians
Growing a Spirit-filled church
ISBN: 978-1-85345-374-8

2 Corinthians
Restoring harmony
ISBN: 978-1-85345-551-3

1 Peter
Good reasons for hope
ISBN: 978-1-78259-088-0

2 Peter
Living in the light of God's promises
ISBN: 978-1-78259-403-1

1 Timothy
Healthy churches –
effective Christians
ISBN: 978-1-85345-291-8

23rd Psalm
The Lord is my shepherd
ISBN: 978-1-85345-449-3

2 Timothy and Titus
Vital Christianity
ISBN: 978-1-85345-338-0

Abraham
Adventures of faith
ISBN: 978-1-78259-089-7

Acts 1–12
Church on the move
ISBN: 978-1-85345-574-2

Acts 13–28
To the ends of the earth
ISBN: 978-1-85345-592-6

Barnabas
Son of encouragement
ISBN: 978-1-85345-911-5

Bible Genres
Hearing what the Bible really says
ISBN: 978-1-85345-987-0

Daniel
Living boldly for God
ISBN: 978-1-85345-986-3

David
A man after God's own heart
ISBN: 978-1-78259-444-4

Ecclesiastes
Hard questions and
spiritual answers
ISBN: 978-1-85345-371-7

Elijah
A man and his God
ISBN: 978-1-85345-575-9

Elisha
A lesson in faithfulness
ISBN: 978-1-78259-494-9

Ephesians
Claiming your inheritance
ISBN: 978-1-85345-229-1

Esther
For such a time as this
ISBN: 978-1-85345-511-7

Fruit of the Spirit
Growing more like Jesus
ISBN: 978-1-85345-375-5

Galatians
Freedom in Christ
ISBN: 978-1-85345-648-0

God's Rescue Plan
Finding God's fingerprints
on human history
ISBN: 978-1-85345-294-9

Great Prayers of the Bible
Applying them to our lives today
ISBN: 978-1-85345-253-6

Haggai
Motivating God's people
ISBN: 978-1-78259-686-8

Hebrews
Jesus – simply the best
ISBN: 978-1-85345-337-3

Hosea
The love that never fails
ISBN: 978-1-85345-290-1

Isaiah 1–39
Prophet to the nations
ISBN: 978-1-85345-510-0

Isaiah 40–66
Prophet of restoration
ISBN: 978-1-85345-550-6

Jacob
Taking hold of God's blessing
ISBN: 978-1-78259-685-1

James
Faith in action
ISBN: 978-1-85345-293-2

Jeremiah
The passionate prophet
ISBN: 978-1-85345-372-4

John's Gospel
Exploring the seven miraculous signs
ISBN: 978-1-85345-295-6

Joseph
The power of forgiveness and reconciliation
ISBN: 978-1-85345-252-9

Joshua 1–10
Hand in hand with God
ISBN: 978-1-85345-542-7

Judges 1–8
The spiral of faith
ISBN: 978-1-85345-681-7

Judges 9–21
Learning to live God's way
ISBN: 978-1-85345-910-8

Luke
A prescription for living
ISBN: 978-1-78259-270-9

Mark
Life as it is meant to be lived
ISBN: 978-1-85345-233-8

Mary
The mother of Jesus
ISBN: 978-1-78259-402-4

Moses
Face to face with God
ISBN: 978-1-85345-336-6

Names of God
Exploring the depths of God's character
ISBN: 978-1-85345-680-0

Nehemiah
Principles for life
ISBN: 978-1-85345-335-9

Parables
Communicating God on earth
ISBN: 978-1-85345-340-3

Philemon
From slavery to freedom
ISBN: 978-1-85345-453-0

Philippians
Living for the sake of the gospel
ISBN: 978-1-85345-421-9

Prayers of Jesus
Hearing His heartbeat
ISBN: 978-1-85345-647-3

Proverbs
Living a life of wisdom
ISBN: 978-1-85345-373-1

Revelation 1–3
Christ's call to the Church
ISBN: 978-1-85345-461-5

Revelation 4–22
The Lamb wins! Christ's final victory
ISBN: 978-1-85345-411-0

Rivers of Justice
Responding to God's call to righteousness today
ISBN: 978-1-85345-339-7

Ruth
Loving kindness in action
ISBN: 978-1-85345-231-4

The Armour of God
Living in His strength
ISBN: 978-1-78259-583-0

The Beatitudes
Immersed in the grace of Christ
ISBN: 978-1-78259-495-6

The Covenants
God's promises and their relevance today
ISBN: 978-1-85345-255-0

The Creed
Belief in action
SBN: 978-1-78259-202-0

The Divine Blueprint
God's extraordinary power in ordinary lives
ISBN: 978-1-85345-292-5

The Holy Spirit
Understanding and experiencing Him
ISBN: 978-1-85345-254-3

The Image of God
His attributes and character
ISBN: 978-1-85345-228-4

The Kingdom
Studies from Matthew's Gospel
ISBN: 978-1-85345-251-2

The Letter to the Colossians
In Christ alone
ISBN: 978-1-855345-405-9

The Letter to the Romans
Good news for everyone
ISBN: 978-1-85345-250-5

The Lord's Prayer
Praying Jesus' way
ISBN: 978-1-85345-460-8

The Prodigal Son
Amazing grace
ISBN: 978-1-85345-412-7

The Second Coming
Living in the light of Jesus' return
ISBN: 978-1-85345-422-6

The Sermon on the Mount
Life within the new covenant
ISBN: 978-1-85345-370-0

Thessalonians
Building Church in changing times
ISBN: 978-1-78259-443-7

The Ten Commandments
Living God's Way
ISBN: 978-1-85345-593-3

The Uniqueness of our Faith
What makes Christianity distinctive?
ISBN: 978-1-85345-232-1

For current prices or to order, visit **www.cwr.org.uk/store**
Available online or from Christian bookshops.

SmallGroup central

All of our small group ideas and resources in one place

Online:

www.smallgroupcentral.org.uk
is filled with free video teaching,
tools, articles and a whole host
of ideas.

On the road:

A range of seminars themed for
small groups can be brought to
your local community. Contact us at
hello@smallgroupcentral.org.uk

In print:

Books, study guides and DVDs
covering an extensive list of themes,
Bible books and life issues.

Log on and find out more at:
www.smallgroupcentral.org.uk

Courses and events

Waverley Abbey College

Publishing and media

Conference facilities

Transforming lives

CWR's vision is to enable people to experience personal transformation through applying God's Word to their lives and relationships.

Our Bible-based training and resources help people around the world to:
• Grow in their walk with God
• Understand and apply Scripture to their lives
• Resource themselves and their church
• Develop pastoral care and counselling skills
• Train for leadership
• Strengthen relationships, marriage and family life and much more.

Our insightful writers provide daily Bible reading notes and other resources for all ages, and our experienced course designers and presenters have gained an international reputation for excellence and effectiveness.

CWR's Training and Conference Centres in Surrey and East Sussex, England, provide excellent facilities in idyllic settings – ideal for both learning and spiritual refreshment.

CWR Applying God's Word
to everyday life and relationships

CWR, Waverley Abbey House,
Waverley Lane, Farnham,
Surrey GU9 8EP, UK

Telephone: **+44 (0)1252 784700**
Email: **info@cwr.org.uk**
Website: **www.cwr.org.uk**

Registered Charity No. 294387
Company Registration No. 1990308